Donald Trump Takes a Dump!

Trump's Verbal Dumps: A Bathroom Companion

By Sabrina Carol

About the Author

Sabrina Carol is a mother of four. Originally from the USA, she now lives in England.

She passionately advocates for creating safe, nurturing environments where children can thrive offline and online.

Sabrina manages her family life while maintaining an impressive 26-year career in cybersecurity. Her professional expertise and personal experiences as a parent give her a unique perspective on the challenges and opportunities of raising children in today's digital age. Sabrina understands parents' complexities when navigating the online world and is deeply committed to empowering families with practical tools, insights, and strategies to enhance safety and resilience.

Throughout her career in cybersecurity, Sabrina has worked with prominent organisations to design and implement systems that protect individuals and businesses from digital threats. Her efforts have consistently been based on the belief that technology should enhance lives, not jeopardise them. By merging this professional knowledge with her role as a mother, Sabrina provides a thoughtful, compassionate approach to her writing, ensuring that every parent feels empowered to guide their children through the ever-changing digital landscape. In her spare time, she enjoys exploring the stunning beauty of the Lake District with her family, often drawing inspiration for her writing from the serene moments in nature.

Table of Contents

Chapter 1:

Introduction – A Golden Throne of Nonsense

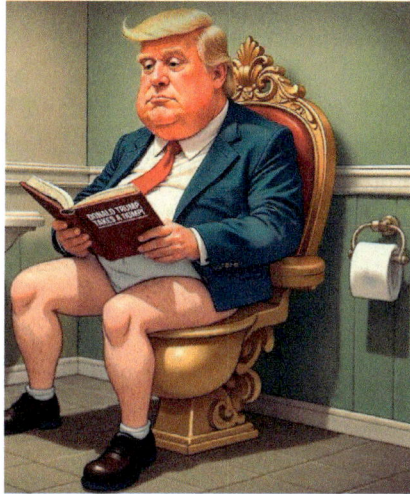

Few men in history have sat on a golden throne. Kings, emperors, and despots have ruled from gilded seats of power, their words bearing the weight of empires. Then there's Donald J. Trump—who not only allegedly owned a literal golden toilet but also managed to turn every public statement into a verbal dump of historical proportions.

This book is not about policies, laws, or political philosophy. That would give too much credit to a man whose most famous legislative contribution is coining the phrase **"Person. Woman. Man. Camera. TV."**

Instead, this is a deep dive into the swirling, nonsensical, and often terrifying whirlpool of Trump's words—his greatest feuds, bizarre obsessions, catastrophic typos, and outright fabrications.

Trump didn't just speak; he **spewed**. He didn't merely communicate; he **unleashed**. His press conferences, rallies, and 3 AM tweets often read less like presidential statements and more like the unfiltered ramblings of a drunk uncle at Thanksgiving dinner. Yet, somehow, they captivated millions, horrified the rest of the world, and made for endless comedy material.

The Stream-of-Consciousness President

Most politicians carefully craft their words. They have speechwriters, strategists, and focus groups, ensuring that every phrase lands just right. Trump had none of that—just a Twitter account (until they took it away), an unwavering belief in his genius, and a vocabulary that made **a third-grade English teacher weep**.

Consider this iconic moment from 2016:

"Look at my African American over here!"

It was a sentence so wildly inappropriate that it was hard to believe it was real. But it was. Trump had spotted a Black supporter in the crowd. Instead, of, you know, *speaking like a normal human being,* he blurted out what sounded like the introduction to a children's book about racial insensitivity.

Or his description of Hurricane Harvey's devastation:

"It's been a wonderful thing. I mean, as tough as this was, it's been a wonderful thing, I think, even for the country to watch and for the world to watch."

Yes, Mr. President. Watching people's homes get washed away was just delightful for everyone.

Then there was his meeting with NATO allies, where he proudly proclaimed:

"I'm a very stable genius."

A phrase that—much like "jumbo shrimp" or "military intelligence"—felt deeply contradictory. Stable geniuses don't generally need to announce their stability or their genius. But Trump was different.

Covfefe and Other Legendary Brain Farts

Trump's verbal missteps weren't just random; they were **legendary**. Even his typos had a life of their own. In May 2017, he tweeted:

"Despite the constant negative press covfefe."

And that was it. A sentence fragment, dropped into the void, never to be explained. Was it a typo? A secret code? A signal to Russian operatives? No one knew.

The White House refused to clarify, claiming that **"the president and a small group of people know exactly what he meant."**

Spoiler: They didn't. No one did.

The internet, however, went **wild**. Within hours, "covfefe" was a meme, a T-shirt slogan, and a symbol of Trump's unique relationship with the English language.

And this was not a one-time event. Trump's Twitter account was **a playground of grammatical disasters**, with classics like:

- **"Hambergers"** (what he fed the Clemson football team after a government shutdown).

- **"No challenge is to great"** (too bad the challenge of basic spelling was one of them).

- **"Barrack Obama"** (he misspelt his predecessor's name *multiple times*).

His inability to form coherent sentences was legendary, even when he wasn't on Twitter. Who could forget his attempt at explaining the American Revolution?

"Our Army manned the air, it rammed the ramparts, it took over the airports, it did everything it had to do."

Yes. The American **Revolutionary War** apparently had **airports**. Someone, please check the history books.

The Art of the (Incoherent) Deal

Trump's ability to twist language into an unrecognisable mess wasn't just limited to Twitter—it bled into **his business deals, his political policies, and his entire presidency.**

For example, his famous border wall promise. First, Mexico was going to pay for it. Then it was *sort of* going to pay for it. Then the American taxpayer would fund it, but it wasn't actually a wall—it was a fence, or maybe a barrier, or possibly just some **steel slats that sort of looked like a wall if you squinted hard enough.**

His trade negotiations weren't much better. He often **bragged** about his negotiation skills but then **insulted** the very people he was supposed to be working with.

- Canada's Prime Minister Justin Trudeau? A "very dishonest" guy.

- Germany's Angela Merkel? She "owes us a lot of money."

- North Korean dictator Kim Jong-un? "We fell in love."

Wait—*what?!*

Yes. Trump **claimed** he and Kim Jong-un exchanged **"beautiful letters"** and had **"fallen in love."** Meanwhile, Kim continued testing nuclear weapons. Ah, diplomacy at its finest.

Why This Book Exists

So, why write a book chronicling Trump's greatest verbal disasters? Because his **words shaped history**— whether we like it or not. His **insults, lies, feuds, and bizarre speeches** dominated headlines for years. And though his presidency may be over (for now), Trumpism isn't going anywhere.

This book is a **bathroom companion**, a **satirical encyclopaedia**, and a **historical nonsense record**. Think of it as the **Rosetta Stone of Trump-speak**—a guide to decoding the **rants, typos, and incoherent monologues** of the most unfiltered president in modern history.

Buckle up. It's going to be a wild ride.

Chapter 2:

"Covfefe" and Other Legendary Brain Farts

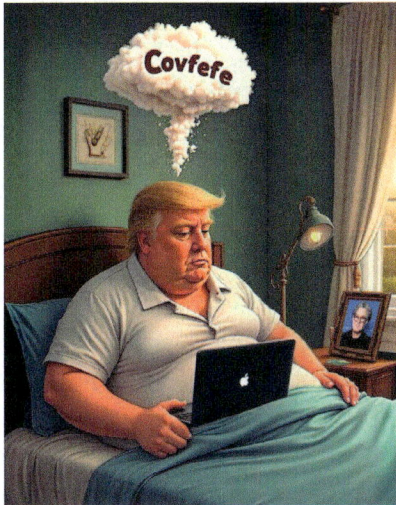

It is **2:47 AM**, and America is once again witness to **presidential history in the making**. The commander-in-chief is **not asleep, strategising, or engaging in statecraft**—he is **doing what he does best**: tweeting.

A few moments later, **the internet explodes**.

"Despite the constant negative press covfefe."

And then—silence. No context. No explanation.

The tweet lingers **for six long hours** before disappearing. By then, the world has **already entered a full-blown crisis of interpretation.**

- **Is "covfefe" a secret nuclear launch code?**
- **A distress signal from the White House bunker?**
- **An accidental summoning of an ancient demon?**
- **Or just the unfortunate result of falling asleep mid-rant?**

As reporters bombard the White House for answers, Trump emerges, **swaggering** with the confidence of a man who has **never second-guessed a single thought in his life.**

"The people who need to know... they already know what it means."

With that, **the mystery deepens.**

A Presidency Built on Verbal Chaos

Most world leaders follow **strict unspoken rules:** speak clearly, think before you talk, and avoid complete nonsense.

Trump, however, **throws these rules out the window.**

Every speech, press conference, and **late-night social media meltdown** is **a high-risk linguistic experiment** where no one—not even Trump himself—knows what will happen next.

For a president, every word matters. **Unless you're Trump, i**n that case, **every word is optional, made up, or a complete accident.**

1. The Great "Person. Woman. Man. Camera. TV." Triumph

It is **a bright day in Washington, D.C.,** and Trump is **beaming with pride. He hasn't just accomplished something incredible**—he has done **something no other world leader has ever dared to boast about.**

Not **winning a war,** not **resolving a significant economic crisis**—but **passing a cognitive test.**

Standing before reporters, he launches into **a complete play-by-play of the event.**

"They ask you to remember five words. Like, let's say, Person. Woman. Man. Camera. TV. Okay? And then, after ten minutes, they ask you to repeat them! And I got it. Perfect. In order."

His **face is glowing** with the pure satisfaction of a child **showing off a macaroni art project.**

The **press stares in horror.**

Sir, you just described a dementia test.

The internet **erupts**. Late-night hosts can't believe their luck. **"Person. Woman. Man. Camera. TV."** is now the **new anthem of a confused presidency.**

And **just like that**, a **new presidential achievement is born.**

2. The "Inject Disinfectant" Incident

The world is facing **a deadly pandemic.** Doctors and scientists are racing to find a cure.

Trump, however, **has a better idea.**

At a **nationally televised briefing**, he turns to his medical experts and says:

"I see the disinfectant, where it knocks it out in a minute. One minute. And is there a way we can do something like that, by injection inside the body?"

The **room freezes**. The **doctors' faces go pale.** The **Clorox PR team collapses on the spot.**

The **next day,** poison control hotlines **are flooded** with calls from Americans asking:

- **"Can I drink bleach?"**
- **"Is Lysol safe as a vaccine?"**

- "If I bathe in hand sanitiser, am I immune?"

The **CDC** is forced to issue an emergency statement:

🚨 **DO NOT DRINK DISINFECTANT.** 🚨

The world **is speechless**. And Trump? **He doubles down.**

"I was being sarcastic," he says, even though **the entire country** saw **his completely serious face** say it **on live TV**.

Science **takes another blow.**

3. The Time He Thought the Revolutionary Army Had Airports

It's **the Fourth of July**, and Trump delivers **a patriotic speech**. The **crowd is ready**.

Then, he drops this **historical bombshell**:

"Our Army manned the air, it rammed the ramparts, it took over the airports, it did everything it had to do."

Wait.

Did… did the Continental Army have **airports**?

In **1776**?

Somewhere, **George Washington is rolling over in his grave**.

Historians **choke on their coffee**. Twitter **goes nuclear**.

Did Paul Revere warn the British with **a Delta Airlines announcement?**

Did Benjamin Franklin **invent WiFi in Terminal B?**

When **confronted with the mistake**, Trump **blamed the teleprompter.**

Of course.

4. "We Fell in Love" – Trump's Strange Love Affair with Kim Jong-Un

Most U.S. presidents **approach diplomacy with caution.**

Trump, however, **approaches it like a contestant on The Bachelor.**

When talking about **North Korean dictator Kim Jong-Un**, Trump **glows like a schoolboy with a crush.**

"We wrote letters. We fell in love."

Fell in love.

With **a dictator.**

The **entire world freezes.** The **CIA chokes on their coffee.** Twitter **explodes.**

Is this **a diplomatic strategy?** Or is **Trump two steps away from sending** Kim Jong-Un a romantic mixtape?

Kim, meanwhile, **continues building nuclear weapons.**

Love hurts.

5. The Never-Ending Feud with the English Language

If there's **one battle Trump always loses,** it's **his war against spelling.**

Some **historic typos:**

- **"Hambergers"** (as in, the meal he served a championship football team).

- **"Unpresidented"** (instead of unprecedented).

- **"Smocking gun"** (instead of smoking gun).

- **"Barrack Obama"** (spelled wrong **multiple times**).

Even **official White House documents** aren't safe.

One memo **urges Americans** to protect their **"Nuclear Arsenal's."**

Grammar teachers **around the country cry themselves to sleep.**

Final Thoughts: A Presidency of Brain Farts

Most presidents leave behind **policies, laws, and legacies.**

Trump leaves behind **typos, bizarre speeches, and surreal moments that historians will be confused for centuries.**

One thing is certain:

We **still have four more years of this.**

Buckle up.

Chapter 3:

All-Time Greatest Feuds – From Rosie to Ron DeSantis

Donald J. Trump is not just **a president**. He is **a full-time feuder**, a **one-man insult factory**, and **the pettiest grudge-holder to ever set foot in the White House**.

Most world leaders negotiate trade deals, improve infrastructure, and maintain **diplomacy**. Trump, however, **spends his days scrolling Twitter (or rather, Truth Social, since he got banned),** screaming at TVs, and thinking up new nicknames for people who mildly annoy him.

His enemy's list is **longer than the receipts at CVS**, featuring **celebrities, world leaders, journalists, former allies, and at least three household appliances that made his hair look bad on live TV.**

A Feud-Fuelled Presidency

Trump doesn't just **fight people**—he **wages full-scale wars**. And once you're on his **list**, you're on it **for life.**

Some feuds **last a few days.** Some **never die.** Some are so **completely random** that you wonder if **Trump just spins a wheel of enemies every morning and picks one at random.**

So buckle up. We're diving into **the most ridiculous, unhinged, and completely unnecessary feuds** that have defined **Trump's presidency, his comeback presidency, and probably his future presidency** from a **Mar-a-Lago golf cart in 2040.**

1. The Rosie O'Donnell Feud – A Grudge That Outlived Most Marriages

Before Trump became **the grudge-holding leader of the free world,** he was **a grudge-holding reality TV star**. And before he feuded **with Republican governors and world leaders,** he was involved in a feud **with a comedian.**

That comedian? **Rosie O'Donnell.**

The war started in **2006,** when Rosie, then a co-host on *The View,* made **the biggest mistake of her life**—she **mocked Trump's business failures, his finances, and, worst of all, his hair.**

For **any other person,** this would have been **a passing joke.**

For Trump?

THIS BECAME HIS PERSONAL 9/11.

- He called her a **"fat little Rosie."**

- He **threatened to sue her** because, of course, he did.

- He went on TV **every chance he got** to remind the world **how much he hated Rosie O'Donnell.**

- He **brought up Rosie** during **presidential debates, rallies,** and **interviews** about entirely unrelated topics.

By **2025**, Rosie O'Donnell is **retired, unbothered, and probably meditating on a beach somewhere.**

Trump? **Still talking about her.**

During a **press briefing on inflation**, a reporter asks, **"Mr. President, what is your administration doing to lower prices for American families?"**

Trump **leans forward, glares at the crowd, and says:**

"You know who doesn't know anything about money? Rosie O'Donnell. TOTAL DISASTER. Just awful."

The press pool **blinks in disbelief.**

Inflation? **No answer.**

Rosie? **Locked and loaded.**

The feud **will never die.** Rosie could **become a nun** tomorrow, and Trump would still **find a way to call her a "nasty woman" in a speech about military funding.**

2. "Meatball Ron" – The War Against Ron DeSantis

If you told **Donald Trump** in 2020 that **Ron DeSantis** would one day be **his greatest Republican enemy,** he would have laughed in your face, called you **a loser,** and probably tried to sell you a red hat.

At one point, **DeSantis was Trump's golden boy,** his **mini-me,** his **Florida apprentice.**

Then, **something unspeakable happened.**

Ron got **a little too confident.**

People started **whispering** that maybe **DeSantis could replace Trump as the Republican leader.**

Maybe **Ron should be president instead.**

BIG. MISTAKE.

Trump, sensing **disloyalty, declares all-out war.**

- **First, he goes for Ron's personality.** Calls him **"dull", "boring",** and **"has the energy of a day-old Big Mac."**

- **Then, he moves to body insults.** Calls him **"Meatball Ron."**

- **Then, he gives him the most awkward nickname in history:** **"Ron DeSanctimonious."**

Nobody knows **what it means**, but it **doesn't matter**.

Trump **says it so much, it sticks**.

By the time **DeSantis finally gives up and retires**, Trump is **still calling him "Meatball Ron"**, even when **Ron isn't even in politics anymore**.

At a **rally about education reform**, Trump suddenly yells:

"MEATBALL RON WAS A FRAUD. TOTAL FRAUD."

A confused supporter in the crowd yells, **"Wait, is he still running?"**

Trump shrugs. **"Doesn't matter. He's a loser."**

And **just like that, DeSantis is erased from history**.

3. Hillary Clinton – Trump's Eternal Villain

Hillary Clinton could **move to Mars**, and Trump **would still blame her for things**.

It's been **a decade since she last ran for office**, but Trump **isn't done fighting her**.

At a **2027 press conference about space exploration**, a reporter asks about **NASA's new moon mission**.

Trump **leans into the mic and says:**

"You know who should be on the moon? Crooked Hillary. Total disgrace. LOCK HER UP."

The room **goes silent.**

Sir, what does this have to do with NASA?

Nothing. But that **doesn't matter.**

4. The "Fake News" Feud – A War Against Reality Itself

Trump's **biggest enemy** isn't a person.

It's **the media.**

From **day one,** he **declares war** on journalism.

- CNN? **Fake news.**
- The New York Times? **"A third-rate paper."**
- Fox News (yes, even them)? **"Too liberal."**
- Reporters who ask real questions? **"Enemies of the people."**

Every press briefing **is the same.**

A journalist asks about **the economy.**

Trump **leans forward and says:**

"You're fake news. Sit down."

The journalist tries again.

"Sir, this is an important—"

"Nope. Fake. Get 'em outta here."

The entire **White House press corps sighs in unison.**

This **will never change.**

Final Thoughts: Feuds Forever

Donald Trump is **not just a president.**

He is **the pettiest man on Earth.**

He will **never let anything go.** He will **never move on.** He will be **98 years old, screaming about Rosie O'Donnell from his nursing home bed.**

And if you think **this chapter is the end of Trump's feuds—**

THINK AGAIN.

The next battle is **just one tweet away.**

Chapter 4:

"We Fell in Love" – Trump's Strange Love Affair with Kim Jong-Un

Ah, love. The thing that makes the world go 'round. The force that has inspired poets, musicians, and Nicholas Sparks novels. The foundation of humanity's greatest stories, from Romeo and Juliet to The Notebook to… whatever it is Donald Trump and Kim Jong-Un have going on.

Yes, folks, of all the bizarre, eyebrow-raising, tinfoil-hat-wearing moments in Trump's presidency, **his baffling bromance with North Korea's Supreme Leader takes the wedding cake.**

Presidents usually **don't** declare their love for **dictators with nuclear weapons,** but then again, **Trump is not most presidents.** Most presidents **negotiate** with world leaders. Trump **flirts** with them.

Ladies and gentlemen, fasten your seatbelts. We're about to take a deep dive into the **most awkward, cringeworthy, and dangerously weird geopolitical romance in modern history.**

Act I: Love at First Nuke

At first, their relationship was **rocky.** You know, like a classic rom-com where the couple **hates each other before realizing they were meant to be.**

Kim Jong-Un started **by calling Trump a "mentally deranged dotard."** Trump, never one to back down from a **mature, rational discussion, clapped back with the Twitter insult of the century:**

"Why would Kim Jong-Un insult me by calling me 'old,' when I would NEVER call him short and fat?"

You see, **this is how nuclear wars start, people.**

It was **the world's first petty, passive-aggressive international Twitter beef.** Kim launches test missiles, Trump **launches tweets,** and **the planet** collectively clenches.

Then, something **magical happens.**

Trump, in **what can only be described as a foreign policy strategy inspired by The Bachelor, decides to woo Kim instead.**

He stops insulting him. He starts sending letters. LOVE letters.

Cue the romantic comedy montage.

Act II: "We Wrote Letters. We Fell in Love."

Folks, picture this. It's **2018,** and Trump is **standing at a rally,** orange glow in full effect, gesturing wildly like he's describing the size of a fish he totally caught.

And then—he **drops** the line that **breaks the internet.**

"We wrote letters. We fell in love."

Wait. Hold up. **What.**

Did the **President of the United States** just **admit to being in a long-distance relationship with a dictator?**

Twitter **immediately combusts.**

One user writes:

"Trump's foreign policy is just a YA novel where the bad boy dictator changes for the quirky American girl."

Another tweets:

"Trump and Kim Jong-Un are like that toxic couple who break up every two weeks but still share a Netflix account."

The world collectively wonders:

- **Is Kim sending Trump mixtapes?**
- **Are they arguing over who says 'I love you' first?**
- **Is this why Melania always looks like she's ready to file divorce papers?**

It gets **better.** Trump **keeps talking about the letters.** He **brags** about them like a teenager showing off texts from their crush.

"He wrote me beautiful letters. They're great letters. I mean, they're like... really beautiful."

Someone needs to check if **Trump is doodling 'Don & Kim 4Ever'** in the margins of his national security briefings.

Act III: When Love Gets Weird (and Nuclear)

At this point, the **relationship** is in **full swing**. Trump is **practically writing Kim's name in the sky**.

There's just **one problem.**

Kim **still has nukes.**

And he's still **testing them.**

It's the **equivalent** of dating someone who **keeps setting your car on fire** but you're like, **"But he wrote me a really sweet text, so we're fine."**

At a press conference, a reporter **bravely** asks, **"Mr. President, aren't you concerned that North Korea is still launching missiles?"**

Trump, with **the confidence of a man who doesn't understand the question but refuses to admit it,** says:

"Oh, he's a tough guy, but you know what? He respects me. And when you have respect, you don't need missiles."

...Sir, that is **not** how missiles work.

Act IV: The Awkward Breakup

Like **all great romances**, Trump and Kim's relationship **eventually hits the rocks.**

Trump starts **losing interest.** Kim, **probably feeling ghosted, starts launching missiles again.**

Trump, trying to **downplay the situation**, says:

"Oh, those are just little missiles. They're very small. It's fine."

EXCUSE ME, SIR.

"LITTLE" missiles?

What are we talking about here, bottle rockets? Roman candles?

The Pentagon **is quietly losing its mind.** Kim **is getting clingy.** Trump **is moving on.**

The love story **ends** not with a **bang,** but with **a whimper and a deleted tweet.**

Act V: Final Thoughts on the World's Weirdest Bromance

Let's review.

Donald Trump, the **President of the United States**, did the following:

- **Slid into Kim Jong-Un's international DMs.**

- **Exchanged "beautiful letters."**

- **Professed his love at a rally.**

- **Ignored nuclear missile tests because of "respect."**

- **Somehow, thought this was a successful diplomatic strategy.**

It's **2027**, and Trump **still won't shut up about it.**

At a press briefing about **gas prices**, Trump suddenly says:

"You know, Kim wrote me some really great letters. I miss those letters. Beautiful handwriting. You don't see that anymore."

A reporter raises a hand.

"Sir, what does this have to do with gas prices?"

Trump **waves them off.**

"Fake news. You wouldn't understand. It's called respect."

Ladies and gentlemen, **we lived through an era where the leader of the free world had a genuine, emotional, probably one-sided love affair with a nuclear-armed dictator.**

This will be in history books.

Historians will look at 2018 and say:

- **"Wait, this actually happened?"**
- **"Did the President really fall for the bad boy dictator?"**
- **"Is it too early to start drinking?"**

And the answer to all of these questions?

Yes. Absolutely yes.

Chapter 5:

The Art of the Incoherent Deal

Ah, business! The great American tradition! The **lifeblood of capitalism!** The **thing Trump pretends to be good at!**

For most people, **making a deal involves logic, strategy, and a basic understanding of math.** For Trump, however, it involves **loud noises, random insults, and walking out of the room when things get complicated.**

Trump has spent **his entire career** telling us he's the **greatest** dealmaker of all time—a **genius businessman** who **turns everything he touches into gold.**

Reality check:

- He bankrupted **casinos.** Let me repeat that. **CASINOS.** Places where **people willingly throw their money away.**

- He ran a **fake university** that scammed students out of thousands of dollars—and **then declared it a success.**

- He started **Trump Steaks**, a business that lasted about as long as a **McDonald's Happy Meal.**

Yet somehow, **he convinces millions of people that he's a financial wizard.** It's like hiring **a guy who burned down a restaurant** to be your **head chef.**

This chapter is a deep dive into **Trump's greatest deals**—and by "greatest," I mean **absolute dumpster fires that he somehow claimed were victories.**

Lesson 1: A Deal is Always a Success, Even When It's a Disaster

Let's start with **Trump University.**

Yes, folks, **Trump once started a university.** A university. The same man who **thinks windmills cause cancer** thought he should be in charge of **higher education.**

The university **had no accreditation, no real professors, and students paid tens of thousands of dollars for a diploma that was about as valuable as a Chuck E. Cheese prize ticket.**

Naturally, **it collapsed.**

The state of New York **sued Trump for fraud.** He **settled for $25 million.**

And what did Trump say?

"It was a tremendous success."

Folks, if **losing a $25 million lawsuit is a success,** then **I'm the Princess of Wales.**

Lesson 2: Trade Wars are Good and Easy to Win (They're Not)

Ah, yes. **The legendary trade war with China.**

Let's break this down like a **bad action movie:**

- Trump **randomly wakes up one morning** and declares a **full-blown trade war with China.**

- He slaps **massive tariffs on Chinese goods,** claiming it will bring **jobs back to America.**

- China **immediately retaliates** because that's **how trade wars work.**

- **Farmers start losing billions** in sales.

- **U.S. companies are forced to raise prices.**

- **Americans end up paying more for everything.**

At a press conference, a reporter asks, **"Mr. President, do you think the trade war is hurting the economy?"**

Trump responds:

"We are winning! We are making so much money! China is paying for everything!"

Sir. **China is not paying for anything.**

That's like **punching yourself in the face and then bragging that your neighbour is in pain.**

By the time **the trade war is over**, the U.S. economy has lost **billions of dollars,** and China **just kept on trucking like nothing happened.**

And what does Trump do?

Declares victory.

Because, folks, **nothing says "winning" like setting your house on fire and congratulating yourself on putting it out.**

Lesson 3: Walk Away and Declare Victory

Trump's **favourite negotiation tactic? Leave the room and pretend you won.**

He used this **brilliant strategy** with **Kim Jong-Un** (see Chapter 4) and again during **his border wall "negotiations."**

Remember the **wall Mexico was supposed to pay for?**

Well, fast forward **four years:**

- **The wall still isn't finished.**

- **The parts that ARE built are falling apart.**

- **Mexico has paid precisely $0.00.**

At a rally, someone asks, **"Mr. President, when will Mexico pay for the wall?"**

Trump smirks and says:

"Oh, they already did. You just don't know it."

Sir, **that is not how money works.**

That's like telling your landlord, **"I already paid rent, you just don't see it yet."**

And just like that, **Trump walks away, declares victory, and leaves everyone confused.**

Lesson 4: The Stock Market is My Mood Ring

One of **Trump's favourite things** to brag about is **the stock market.**

Whenever the market **goes up**, Trump takes **full credit.**

Whenever it **goes down**, it's **Obama's fault.**

It's like saying:

- **"I made the sun rise today."**
- **"I am personally responsible for gravity."**

- "The seasons change because I tell them to."

At one rally, Trump says:

"If Joe Biden wins, the stock market will **CRASH**. It'll be the worst crash ever. Worse than the Great Depression. Worse than the dinosaurs. Worse than... I don't know, it'll just be really bad!"

And then **Biden wins.**

And the stock market **keeps going up.**

And Trump is like: **"Fake news."**

If **Trump** had his way, he'd take credit for oxygen.

Lesson 5: If a Deal Fails, Blame Someone Else

Trump's **golden rule of business?**

If something fails, IT'S NEVER HIS FAULT.

- **Trump Casinos go bankrupt?** Not his fault.

- **Trump Steaks flop?** Not his fault.

- **Trump's Atlantic City hotel is now an abandoned wasteland?** NOT HIS FAULT.

At one press briefing, a reporter asks, **"Mr. President, do you take responsibility for the economic downturn?"**

Trump, without blinking, says:

"I take no responsibility. None."

The **PRESIDENT. OF. THE. UNITED. STATES.**

I have seen **kindergarteners take more responsibility for knocking over a juice box.**

Final Exam: What Have We Learned?

After five lessons in **Trumpian deal-making**, here's what you should take away:

1. **Every deal succeeds, even when it's a catastrophe.**

2. **If you lose a trade war, just declare victory and move on.**

3. **Walking away from negotiations randomly makes you look powerful. (It doesn't.)**

4. **If you promise someone else will pay for something, and they don't just pretend they did.**

5. **If anything fails, blame Obama.**

Ladies and gentlemen, **this has been The Art of the Incoherent Deal**—the **only** business strategy where **failure is success, losing is winning, and logic is entirely optional.**

Now, if you'll excuse me, I need a drink.

Chapter 6:

Tiny Hands, Big Words (And Bigger Lies)

Ah, politics! The ancient and noble art of **saying things that sound important but mean absolutely nothing.** Now, normally, a politician will **bend the truth a little,** you know, like when you tell your boss you were "stuck in traffic" but really you just didn't want to get out of bed.

But then came Trump.

This man doesn't just **lie**—he lies like he's **competing for a gold medal in the Olympics of nonsense.** If Pinocchio had Trump's ability to fabricate reality, his nose would have **wrapped around the Earth twice** and been **classified as a new planet by NASA.**

You see, Trump **lies with confidence.** He says things so **wildly untrue, so detached from reality,** that you start questioning if maybe **YOU'RE the crazy one.** He could **look up at a blue sky and declare it purple,** and within an hour, **half of America would be selling T-shirts that say "The Sky is Purple - Deal With It."**

So grab some popcorn, hold onto your critical thinking skills for dear life, and let's take a **whirlwind tour** through the most **insane, reality-bending, brain-melting statements ever uttered by a sitting U.S. president.**

Lesson 1: When in Doubt, Just Make Stuff Up

Alright, let's start with an **absolute classic.** Trump wakes up one morning, walks outside, looks at the crowd for his **presidential inauguration,** and says:

"This was the biggest crowd in history! Bigger than Obama's. Bigger than anyone's! People were crying! Grown men were crying! The biggest crowd the world has ever seen!"

Now, we have **PHOTOGRAPHS.** We have **satellite images.** We have **eyewitness accounts.** And all of them say the same thing:

The crowd was... meh.

It wasn't **terrible,** but let's just say there were **more empty spots than at a Nickelback concert on a Tuesday.**

And when a reporter **dared to mention the actual crowd size,** Trump **lost his mind.**

"LIES! FAKE NEWS! THE MEDIA IS CORRUPT!"

Sir, we can **see the photos.** You are **literally standing in front of the evidence.** This is like getting caught **cheating on a test while holding the answer sheet in your hand** and saying, **"I didn't cheat. The answer sheet cheated."**

Lesson 2: Science is Optional

Trump **doesn't just lie about normal things like crowd sizes and polls.** Oh no, **he goes straight for science.**

Let's talk about **Hurricane Dorian.**

One day, Trump **mistakenly claims** that Alabama is in the path of a hurricane. The National Weather Service **immediately corrects him.**

Now, what does a **normal person do** when they make a mistake?

Option A: Admit they were wrong.

Option B: Ignore it and move on.

Trump **chooses Option C: DRAW A NEW PATH ON A WEATHER MAP WITH A SHARPIE.**

Let me say that again. **THE PRESIDENT TOOK A MARKER AND LITERALLY DREW A FAKE PATH FOR A HURRICANE.**

This is not **a joke.** This **actually happened.**

Scientists across America had **meltdowns.** Weather reporters **lost their minds.** People in Alabama were like, **"Wait, should we be evacuating or is the president just doodling?"**

This is like if a doctor **looked at your X-ray**, saw a fractured leg, and just **grabbed a Sharpie and drew over it**, saying, **"Look! No break! All better!"**

Lesson 3: If It's Too Crazy, Just Double Down

Here's another classic: **Windmills cause cancer.**

One day, Trump is **rambling about energy policy**, and suddenly, **out of nowhere**, he just casually drops:

"Windmills cause cancer."

EXCUSE ME, SIR?!

The entire **scientific community collectively facepalms.** Cancer researchers **start sobbing into their lab coats.** Meanwhile, Trump supporters are **nodding like he just solved the Da Vinci Code.**

A journalist asks, **"Mr. President, what evidence do you have?"**

Trump, without missing a beat:

"A lot of people are talking about it."

SIR. **WHO ARE THESE PEOPLE?**

Are we talking about **scientists? Doctors?** Or are we talking about **Larry from Facebook who thinks toothpaste is a government conspiracy?**

This is like if someone said, **"Unicorns are real,"** and when you ask **for proof,** they say, **"A lot of people are talking about it."**

Lesson 4: If You Get Caught Lying, Lie Bigger

Let's talk about one of Trump's **favorite** tricks: **When caught in a lie, just tell an even BIGGER lie.**

Example: Trump once claimed **his father was born in Germany.**

Fact-checkers: **"No, sir, your father was born in New York."**

Trump: **"No, no, no, he was definitely born in Germany."**

Sir. We have birth certificates. We have census records. We have ANCESTRY.COM.

This is like getting caught sneaking cookies and **instead of admitting it, doubling down and saying,**

"I didn't eat the cookies! In fact, there WERE NO COOKIES. COOKIES HAVE NEVER EXISTED."

And what happens? **His followers eat it up!**

Somewhere, fact-checkers are **crying into their keyboards, wondering why they even bother.**

Lesson 5: If Nothing Works, Just Call It Fake News

Trump's **ultimate defense against facts?**

Just call everything fake.

- **Mueller Report?** Fake.

- **Impeachment?** Fake.

- **Polls showing him losing?** FAKE NEWS!

At one point, he even **yelled at Fox News for being too liberal.**

FOX NEWS. The **same** Fox News that spent years **hyping him up like a WWE character.**

Imagine being **so detached from reality** that you turn on **your own personal cheerleaders** because **they said ONE thing you didn't like.**

Final Thoughts: Lies So Big They Need Their Own ZIP Code

At this point, fact-checkers are **on life support.** Journalists are **aging in dog years.** Scientists are developing migraines that can only be cured by permanent retirement.

Because here's **the real secret** to Trump's lies:

He doesn't care if they're true.

If he says it **enough times, loudly enough, with enough confidence, people will believe it.**

And THAT, ladies and gentlemen, **is the true Art of the Deal.**

The deal is reality itself.

Trump **sells** a version of the world that doesn't exist, and somehow, **people buy it.**

Now, if you'll excuse me, I need **to go lie down in a dark room and rethink my life choices.**

Chapter 7:

Stormy Weather – A Porn Star, a President, and a Whole Lot of Tweets

Act I: The Courtroom Circus

So, folks, you'd think after **getting arrested, humiliated, and meme'd into eternity**, Trump would

lay low for a while, maybe take a quiet vacation, do some deep reflection?

HA! Have you met this man?

Oh no, he **takes his legal troubles and turns them into a full-blown reality show.**

We're talking:

- **Rallies outside the courthouse**

- **MAGA hats that say "LOCK ME UP!" (on sale for $49.99)**

- **An actual speech comparing his arrest to Nelson Mandela and Martin Luther King Jr.**

SIR.

Trump standing in front of his supporters, doing his best MLK impression:

"I HAVE A DREAM… that one day, a billionaire can pay off a porn star without consequences!"

And then **he walks into court like he's strutting down the red carpet,** waving at people like he's at a WWE event, while his lawyers are behind him **sweating like they just took the bar exam 30 minutes ago.**

And folks, if you thought **Trump in the courtroom would be a serious, dignified affair**, you clearly haven't been paying attention.

Because this trial turns into a straight-up Looney Tunes episode.

- Trump scowls at the judge like a toddler who just got told "no cookies before dinner."

- He keeps interrupting his own lawyers to "correct" them (and somehow makes his case worse).

- At one point, he demands to "testify" but is stopped because he literally CANNOT REMEMBER WHAT HIS OWN DEFENSE IS.

Meanwhile, Stormy Daniels is just **sitting in the back of the courtroom sipping her iced coffee like a queen** because she **KNOWS** she already won.

Act II: The Verdict Is In – And So Are the Jokes

The jury goes into **deliberation**.

The world waits.

Fox News anchors **are praying on air.** Sean Hannity is **physically sweating like a guy who just lost his life savings at a blackjack table.**

And then…

GUILTY.

The **FIRST U.S.** president to be convicted in a criminal case.

You'd think this would be **rock bottom.**

BUT NO.

Trump **IMMEDIATELY** goes on Truth Social and posts in all caps:

"TOTAL WITCH HUNT! THE FAKE NEWS MEDIA IS AGAINST ME! STORMY DANIELS SHOULD BE ARRESTED! I AM A POLITICAL PRISONER! LET ME OUT!!!"

Sir. **You are posting from your golden toilet.**

Meanwhile, Stormy Daniels, after **publicly wrecking a former president, goes on a nationwide comedy tour.**

Let me say that again: **She literally goes on a comedy tour.**

This woman **turns her lawsuit into a STAND-UP ACT.**

She is out here **on stage, telling jokes about Trump's tiny hands and bad sex game,** while Trump is pacing around Mar-a-Lago, still tweeting about her six years later.

THIS IS THE FUNNIEST TIMELINE.

Act III: The Never-Ending Grudge

At this point, **you would think Trump would just MOVE ON.**

The man **is running for president AGAIN.** You'd think he would **focus on that,** maybe try to, oh I don't know, **convince voters that he's not a criminal.**

But no.

Instead, **he is STILL ranting about Stormy Daniels.**

At a **2027 campaign rally,** a supporter asks a question about **inflation.**

Trump pauses, leans into the mic, and says:

"You know who's bad with money? STORMY DANIELS! She should be in jail, folks. JAIL."

The crowd goes **silent.**

Sir, what does this have to do with inflation?!

Stormy, of course, **fires back on Twitter (because unlike him, she's still allowed on there).**

"Imagine still being obsessed with me after all these years. Move on, dude. It's embarrassing."

BOOM.

KO.

Final Thoughts: The Most Absurd Scandal in U.S. History

This scandal **will never die.**

Future history books will have an entire **chapter dedicated to Trump vs. Stormy.**

College professors will **struggle to explain this without laughing.**

Historians in **100 years** will look at this mess and say:

- "Wait, did this actually happen?"
- "Did the President of the United States really go to court over a porn star hush money payment?"
- "Did the leader of the free world actually call her 'Horseface' on Twitter?"
- "Why did America let this man be in charge of nuclear codes?"

And the answer to **all of these questions?**

YES. YES. YES. AND NOBODY KNOWS.

Chapter 8:

FAKE NEWS! The War on Reality

Ah, journalism! The noble art of truth-telling! The fourth estate! The guardian of democracy!

But wait! Enter the challenger! A wild, orange-tinted, Twitter-obsessed billionaire appears!

Trump doesn't just **dislike the press**—oh no, my friends. He **declares all-out war on it** like he's starring in some kind of action movie titled *Fake News: The Trump Reckoning*.

Every time CNN reports on something factual, **he foams at the mouth like a rabid raccoon in a gold-plated trash can.** Every time a journalist asks a question, **he squints, huffs, and puffs like a sentient Cheeto trying to blow the White House down.**

And his battle cry?

"FAKE NEWS!"

A phrase he shouts more than Melania shouts **"DON'T TOUCH ME!"**

So grab some popcorn, folks, because this is **the most ridiculous, mind-melting, truth-warping war against reality the world has ever seen!**

Act I: FAKE NEWS! FAKE NEWS! EVERYWHERE!

Imagine this: **Trump is walking through the White House.** A journalist asks:

"Mr. President, what's your plan to fix the economy?"

Trump stares at them like they just **called Ivanka ugly.** He slowly removes his MAGA hat, straightens his tie, leans into the mic, and proudly declares:

"FAKE QUESTION!"

What?

Sir, that's not how words work!

This is the same man who once **tried to convince us the sky was green just because someone on Fox News said so.**

• **Unemployment is up?** FAKE NEWS!

• **He spelled "unprecedented" as "unpresidented"?** FAKE NEWS!

• **The sun rises in the east?** FAKE NEWS, IT'S A HOAX!

Folks, **he's not just rejecting news—he's rejecting physics.** If Trump had been around during the invention of gravity, **he would've tweeted, "FAKE LAW! VERY UNFAIR! I AM NOW FLOATING!"**

Act II: The CNN Blood Feud (A Rivalry for the Ages)

Now, we all know Trump hates CNN **more than he hates vegetables.**

CNN could report that **water is wet**, and Trump would **rage-tweet in all caps:**

"FAKE NEWS! VERY DISHONEST! I KNOW WATER, I HAVE THE BEST WATER! IT'S TREMENDOUS! ASK ANYONE! SAD!"

At one point, **he banned CNN's Jim Acosta from the White House.**

Why? **Because Acosta asked a follow-up question.**

A FOLLOW-UP QUESTION.

That's like getting banned from a McDonald's drive-thru because you asked for extra ketchup.

Trump points at Acosta like an emperor sentencing a gladiator to death.

"YOU'RE A RUDE, TERRIBLE PERSON! SECURITY, TAKE HIM AWAY!"

Meanwhile, dictators across the world are watching this on TV, nodding, saying, **"We like this guy. He gets it."**

Act III: Trump vs. Fox News—A BETRAYAL!

Oh, but wait! There's **a twist!**

For **years**, Fox News was Trump's **BFF.** They covered him with the enthusiasm of **a middle schooler talking about their first crush.**

But the moment **Fox News fact-checked him ONCE,** Trump **lost his mind.**

He rage-tweeted:

"FOX NEWS HAS GONE LIBERAL! VERY DISHONEST! NOW I ONLY WATCH OAN AND SOME GUY NAMED BOB WHO LIVESTREAMS FROM HIS GARAGE."

Imagine being so **unhinged** that **even FOX NEWS is like, "Alright, buddy, this is a bit much."**

Act IV: The "Very Tough" Press Conferences (Or: A Live WWE Event)

Most presidents hold press conferences that are **informative, serious, and boring enough to make you fall asleep mid-sentence.**

Trump's press conferences?

They were professional wrestling matches with fewer chairs being thrown but way more mental gymnastics.

The moment a journalist asked something difficult, **Trump would puff out his chest like a rooster on Viagra and start verbally body-slamming them.**

Journalist: "Mr. President, why did you tweet that Mexico was paying for the wall when they're not?"

Trump: "EXCUSE ME? EXCUSE ME? SIT DOWN! YOU'RE RUDE! VERY RUDE! NEXT QUESTION!"

That's it. That's his entire **debate strategy.**

- **Step 1: Shout "EXCUSE ME" at full volume.**

- **Step 2: Talk over the journalist.**

- **Step 3: Call them a "loser."**

- **Step 4: Declare victory and leave.**

That's not a press briefing, **that's a Thanksgiving dinner argument with your drunk uncle.**

Act V: The Sharpie Incident (Or: When Reality Didn't Cooperate, So He Drew a New One)

Ah yes, **one of the greatest moments in the history of presidential nonsense.**

Hurricane Dorian is approaching. The National Weather Service announces **it's NOT going to hit Alabama.**

Trump, of course, **says Alabama is TOTALLY in danger.**

The weather experts correct him.

And what does Trump do?

DOES HE ADMIT HE'S WRONG? NOPE.

HE TAKES A SHARPIE AND LITERALLY DRAWS A NEW PATH FOR THE HURRICANE.

This man **tried to edit a weather forecast with a MARKER** like a kid forging their report card.

Meteorologists were **losing their minds.** Scientists **were screaming into pillows.** And somewhere, **a poor White House staffer was Googling "how to fake your own death to avoid embarrassment."**

Act VI: ALTERNATIVE FACTS!

Ah, **the moment America finally gave up on reality.**

Kellyanne Conway, Trump's most loyal spin doctor, **was asked why Sean Spicer lied about Trump's inauguration crowd size.**

And instead of just **admitting the truth,** she says:

"We have ALTERNATIVE FACTS."

I'm sorry, WHAT?!

FACTS AREN'T OPTIONAL, KELLYANNE.

This is like telling your math teacher, **"Actually, 2+2 is 97. It's an ALTERNATIVE ANSWER."**

This is like saying, **"I'm not late for work—I'm on an ALTERNATIVE SCHEDULE."**

At this point, **reality is officially broken.**

Final Thoughts: The President Who Lost a War Against Reality

After four years of screaming **"FAKE NEWS" at every fact he didn't like,** here's what we learned:

- **Trump thinks news is only real if it makes him look good.**

- **If you question him, you're "rude" and "a terrible person."**

- **If facts don't match his version of reality, he'll draw a new one with a Sharpie.**

- **If all else fails, scream "FAKE NEWS" and run away.**

Ladies and gentlemen, **this has been the most ridiculous war on truth in human history.**

Final score?

Reality: 1

Trump: Banned from Twitter and still mad about it.

And honestly? **That feels about right.**

Chapter 9:

The Science (or Lack Thereof) of Donald Trump

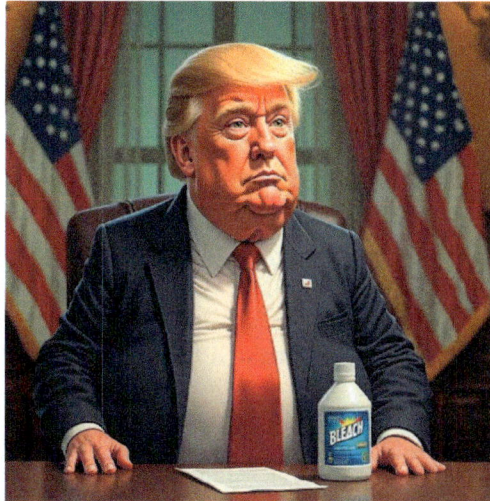

Ah, **science!** That beautiful thing that gave us **electricity, modern medicine, and the ability to Google whether that weird bump on your leg is a spider bite or the first sign of your body completely shutting down.**

Science has done **amazing things for humanity**, but for Donald J. Trump? Oh no, my friends. **Science is the enemy.**

Gravity? Suspicious.

Climate change? A Chinese hoax.

Vaccines? Maybe, maybe not, who knows, let's inject bleach and find out!

See, when most world leaders **don't understand science,** they do the responsible thing: **They listen to experts.**

Trump? Oh, no.

This man **thinks science is a conspiracy, a personal insult, and, worst of all, BORING.** He treats experts like **they just spoiled the ending of his favorite movie.**

So buckle up, kids, because we're about to take a wild, unhinged ride through **Trump vs. Science—The Dumbest Battle in Human History.**

Act I: The President Who Fought a Hurricane (And Lost)

Let's start with **one of Trump's greatest battles against reality—Hurricane Dorian.**

The year is **2019.** The National Weather Service **clearly states** that the hurricane **WILL NOT hit Alabama.**

Trump, for some reason, **wakes up and tweets:**

"HURRICANE DORIAN HEADING STRAIGHT FOR ALABAMA. BE SAFE!"

Meteorologists across America **spit out their coffee.** The National Weather Service **panics.** Alabama residents **start boarding up their windows like a scene from The Purge.**

Within minutes, **scientists rush to correct him.**

So does Trump do the **normal thing** and say, "Oops, my bad"?

NOPE.

Trump **grabs a Sharpie, LITERALLY DRAWS A NEW PATH ON A WEATHER MAP,** and tells the world:

"SEE? I WAS RIGHT!"

SIR.

YOU CANNOT REDRAW A HURRICANE.

THAT IS NOT HOW WEATHER WORKS.

At this point, **scientists start chain-smoking.** The Sharpie industry **sees record-breaking sales.** Somewhere in Alabama, a farmer is yelling at his TV, **"SOMEBODY PLEASE TAKE HIS MARKERS AWAY!"**

Folks, **this is how five-year-olds cheat at board games.** If Trump played Monopoly, **he'd draw new properties on the board and insist he owns them.**

Act II: The Time He Declared War on Windmills

Ah, **windmills.**

Harmless, right? **Just big, spinny things that make clean energy.**

WRONG.

To Trump, **windmills are the DEVIL.**

One day, out of nowhere, **he declares:**

"WINDMILLS CAUSE CANCER."

I'm sorry, WHAT?

Sir, what kind of Scooby-Doo nonsense is this?

Cancer? FROM WIND?

Is there a **secret radioactive gust of death we don't know about?**

Scientists are **screaming into their hands.** The entire **medical community collapses.** People who spent **20 years studying oncology now need therapy.**

Meanwhile, Trump **continues, doubling down:**

"They kill all the birds. The worst thing for birds. Terrible."

Oh, REALLY?

You know what else kills birds?

- **Cars.**
- **Cats.**
- **Buildings.**
- **YOUR ENTIRE DAMN PRESIDENCY.**

But no, folks, **forget oil spills, pollution, or deforestation.** The real enemy? **The windmill outside your grandma's house.**

Act III: The "Inject Bleach" Disaster

And now, folks, we arrive at **the greatest moment in presidential science history.**

April 23, 2020. A day that will live in **medical infamy.**

COVID-19 is raging. People are looking for answers. **Doctors, scientists, and medical professionals** are working around the clock.

And then, **Trump walks into a press briefing.**

He looks at his experts, nods confidently, and then casually suggests:

"Maybe we can inject disinfectant into the body? Like, clean it out from the inside?"

SILENCE.

The room collectively stops breathing.

Somewhere, **Dr. Fauci ages 20 years on the spot.**

The **Clorox PR team faints.** The **Lysol hotline gets flooded with calls.** Poison control issues an emergency warning: **"FOR THE LOVE OF GOD, DO NOT DRINK BLEACH."**

Meanwhile, Trump is **standing there like he just solved cancer.**

"Maybe light? Can we put UV light inside people? Someone should look into this."

SIR.

THE SUN IS FREE. GO OUTSIDE.

At this point, **science packs up its bags and leaves the country.**

And when people start calling him out for suggesting a DIY bleach injection, does Trump take responsibility?

NOPE.

"I WAS BEING SARCASTIC!"

Sir.

You said it with a straight face.

You looked the DOCTORS in the eye.

Nobody is injecting bleach as a joke.

This is like **lighting your house on fire and then saying, "Haha, I was just kidding, guys."**

Act IV: The Great COVID Cover-Up

Now, let's talk about **Trump's pandemic strategy.**

At first, he **completely ignores the virus.**

Then, when people start **dying**, does he take action?

NOPE.

Instead, he **starts giving medical advice based on... vibes.**

He **claims the virus will disappear "like a miracle."**

A MIRACLE.

This man thought **COVID was a seasonal flu mixed with a magic trick.**

Then he suggests:

- **"It's not that bad."**

- "It'll be gone by Easter."

- "We have it under control."

Meanwhile, **hospitals are overflowing, and doctors are yelling, "WE DON'T HAVE IT UNDER CONTROL!"**

Trump sees this and says, **"Fake news."**

Yes, folks, **the virus that was literally killing people was now fake news.**

Act V: The Time He Said Climate Change Was Fake Because It Was Cold One Day

Trump, on a winter morning:

"It's cold outside. Where's global warming?"

Sir.

Sir.

SIR.

That's like **saying world hunger isn't real because you just ate a cheeseburger.**

Science **is weeping.** Meteorologists are **quitting their jobs.** The planet is **physically cringing.**

Final Thoughts: Trump vs. Science—The Most Embarrassing Fight in History

Trump has **lost many battles.**

- The battle against windmills.
- The battle against Sharpie-proof hurricanes.
- The battle against bleach being "a good idea."

But his **greatest defeat?**

The battle against reality itself.

Scientists **tried to educate him.**

Doctors **tried to correct him.**

Meteorologists **tried to stop him from drawing on their damn maps.**

BUT IT DIDN'T MATTER.

Trump looked **logic straight in the face** and said, **"YOU'RE FAKE NEWS."**

And **THAT,** my friends, is why scientists everywhere still wake up screaming.

Chapter 10:

Witch Hunts, Hoaxes, and Total Exonerations

Ah, **witch hunts!**

The phrase Trump has used so many times, **if he had a nickel for every time he said it, he'd have enough money to actually be a billionaire!**

Folks, when a normal person is accused of something, they do **one of three things:**

1. **If they're innocent**, they calmly provide evidence.

2. **If they're guilty**, they either apologize or lawyer up.

3. **If they're Donald Trump**, they SCREAM "WITCH HUNT!" into the nearest microphone, FLAIL THEIR ARMS like one of those inflatable tube men outside a car dealership, and TWEET IN ALL CAPS at 3 AM while rage-eating McDonald's.

"TOTAL EXONERATION!" he shouts, as the FBI raids his house.

"NO COLLUSION!" he insists, as half his inner circle gets fitted for orange jumpsuits.

"THIS IS THE GREATEST INJUSTICE IN HISTORY!" he howls, as historians drop their books and scream, **"SIR, WE HAVE HAD ACTUAL WARS."**

Oh, buckle up, folks, because we are about to take **a high-speed, chaos-fueled ride** through **Trump's greatest hoaxes, conspiracies, and imaginary injustices.**

Act I: The Russia Investigation— Collusion or Just a Weird Bromance with Putin?

Ah, Russia. The country Trump **loves more than he loves Diet Coke.**

From **day one**, people start asking:

"Hey, did Trump's campaign work with Russia to help him win the 2016 election?"

And Trump? Oh, Trump **responds with the subtlety of a car alarm in a library.**

"NO COLLUSION! I DON'T EVEN KNOW RUSSIA! NEVER MET HER!"

Sir. **Russia is a country, not a woman you met at a Vegas casino.**

And then the evidence starts **piling up** like a hoarder's basement:

- Trump's campaign members? **Meeting with Russian operatives in secret.**

- Russian hackers? **Messing with U.S. election systems and spreading fake news.**

- Trump himself? **Literally BEGGING Russia to hack Hillary Clinton's emails ON LIVE TELEVISION.**

Folks, this isn't a **witch hunt**. This is **a full-blown detective show where the suspect is covered in fingerprints, standing over the body, holding the murder weapon, screaming, "I DIDN'T DO IT!"**

And then comes **the Mueller Report.**

Does Trump sit down, read it, and try to clear his name?

NOPE.

He **waves his tiny hands** and shouts:

"TOTAL EXONERATION!"

Sir, the report literally says, "This is NOT an exoneration."

At this point, **even dictionaries are suing him for defamation.**

Act II: The Impeachment Trial—A Perfect Call or a Drunk Dial to a Dictator?

Oh, **impeachment!**

That thing that happens when **a president does something SO BAD that Congress actually looks up from their lobbyist checks and says, "Should we do something about this?"**

And Trump? **Oh, he got impeached TWICE.** That's right—he's the McDonald's of impeachments. **Billions and billions served.**

Let's focus on **the first one.**

The year is **2019. Trump picks up the phone.**

Who does he call? **His lawyer? A general? His wife?**

NOPE.

The President of Ukraine.

And does he talk about **diplomacy? Trade relations? World peace?**

NOPE.

He **pressures Ukraine to dig up dirt on Joe Biden.**

LIVE. ON THE PHONE.

This is not Watergate. This is Idiotgate.

This is like **calling your neighbor and saying, "Hey, while you're at my barbecue, could you also burn down my ex-wife's house?"**

So Congress **impeaches him.** And Trump, in response, **holds a 45-minute rally speech screaming, "HOAX! HOAX! GREATEST HOAX EVER!"**

Sir, **this is not an episode of Scooby-Doo.**

And then the Senate **lets him off the hook.** Why? Because, apparently, **being rich and orange means never facing consequences.**

At this point, **even the Constitution is crying.**

Act III: The Big Lie—An Election So Stolen, Even Dora the Explorer Couldn't Find It

Fast forward to **2020.** Trump is **running for re-election,** and things aren't looking great.

Then, **the votes start coming in.** And oh, does he **LOSE.**

And what does Trump do? **Admit defeat like a grown-up?**

NOPE.

He **throws a tantrum so massive it registers on the Richter scale.**

- **Mail-in ballots? FAKE.**
- **Voting machines? HACKED!**
- **Poll workers? SECRET ANTIFA AGENTS!**
- **Every state he lost? "TOTALLY CORRUPT!"**

- Every state he won? **"VERY HONEST. BEST ELECTION EVER."**

This is like **playing Monopoly,** losing, and then flipping the board over, screaming, **"THIS WHOLE GAME IS A FRAUD!"**

And oh, the lawsuits! **DOZENS OF THEM.**

Trump's legal team, led by **Rudy "I'm Melting" Giuliani,** takes the case to court.

Out of **60+ lawsuits, guess how many they won?**

ONE.

That's like going to a casino, gambling your life savings, and winning a free drink.

And even after **Biden is sworn in,** Trump STILL won't let it go.

He's out here in **2027,** still ranting, still crying, still insisting **he's the real president.**

Sir, **you lost years ago. Please, go home.**

Act IV: January 6th—The Dumbest Coup Attempt in History

Oh boy, folks, **here it is.** The moment Trump's presidency **goes FULL CARTOON VILLAIN.**

January 6, 2021. The day America learned **what happens when you let Facebook uncles believe conspiracy theories for too long.**

Trump, in a speech full of **spit-fueled rage**, tells his supporters:

"MARCH TO THE CAPITOL! FIGHT LIKE HELL!"

And folks, they **LISTEN.**

Thousands of MAGA die-hards storm the U.S. Capitol like **they're starring in a poorly organized action movie.**

And what does Trump do?

Does he **try to stop it?**

NOPE.

He **watches it on TV like it's the damn Super Bowl.**

And when people tell him **"Sir, you need to tell them to stop,"** he FINALLY tweets:

"Go home. We love you. You're very special."

Sir, **THIS IS NOT A PRESCHOOL PLAYDATE.**

Final Thoughts: The Most Investigated Man in History

Trump has been **investigated, impeached, sued, arrested, and fact-checked more than anyone in U.S. history.**

And every time, **he screams "WITCH HUNT!"**

Sir, **if 500 people accuse you of being guilty, MAYBE YOU DID SOMETHING WRONG.**

At this rate, **he'll be on trial DURING his next campaign.**

Picture it now:

"Ladies and gentlemen, I am the only candidate running LIVE from a prison cell! Vote Trump 2028! Total exoneration!"

And honestly? **That seems about right.**

Chapter 11:

Truth Social – The New Twitter, Same Old Crap

Ah, social media! The place where we all **argue with strangers, post pictures of food no one cares about, and accidentally like our crush's selfie from 2012.**

For normal people, it's a place to **connect, share, and occasionally regret everything they've ever posted.**

For Donald J. Trump? **It's a battlefield.**

See, Trump doesn't just **use social media.**

He **inhabits it.**

He **thrives in it.**

He **tweets the way a toddler throws a tantrum in a Walmart.**

And when Twitter had the **audacity**—the **gall**—to finally **ban him after January 6th,** did Trump move on?

Did he take the high road?

NOPE.

He **created his own damn platform!**

Ladies and gentlemen, welcome to **Truth Social—the only social media site where reality goes to die, and every post sounds like it was written in an all-caps fever dream.**

Buckle up, because we are about to dive into **the digital dumpster fire that is Trump's personal Twitter knockoff.**

Act I: The Birth of Truth Social – Or, The Time Trump Rage-Quit the Internet

Picture it: **January 2021.** Trump has been **kicked off Twitter, Facebook, Instagram, and probably even MySpace.**

He is FUMING.

He is **pacing the golden halls of Mar-a-Lago,** clutching his **Diet Coke with two hands,** screaming at his staff:

"HOW DARE THEY SILENCE ME?! I AM THE BEST TWEETER! NO ONE TWEETS LIKE ME! I'M LIKE SHAKESPEARE WITH A SMARTPHONE!"

His aides, who have been **tuning him out for four years, nod and pretend to take notes.**

Then, **a lightbulb moment.**

What if he **made his own Twitter?**

Yes! **A new platform!**

One where **no one fact-checks him!**

One where **no one can kick him off!**

One where **he is the KING OF POSTS!**

And thus, **Truth Social was born.**

Act II: The Launch – A Disaster of Epic Proportions

You'd think, for a guy who **ran the country (poorly) and allegedly is a genius businessman (he isn't),** that he'd make sure his **big new social media platform actually worked.**

Oh no, folks.

The launch of **Truth Social** was **such a colossal train wreck that even Elon Musk was like, "Wow, this is bad."**

Here's what happened:

- **On day one, the app crashes immediately.**
- **Half the users can't even sign up.**
- **The ones who do sign up get stuck on a waitlist longer than the line at the DMV.**
- **The site has fewer features than a 2003 flip phone.**

Meanwhile, Trump is on stage at a rally, proudly announcing:

"WE HAVE BUILT THE GREATEST SOCIAL MEDIA SITE EVER. PEOPLE ARE SAYING IT'S EVEN BETTER THAN TWITTER.

MAYBE EVEN BETTER THAN THE INTERNET ITSELF!"

Sir.

Your website is literally on fire.

At this point, **even his most devoted fans are thinking, "Maybe I should just go back to Facebook."**

Act III: The Rules of Truth Social – Or, How to Get Banned from a Website with No Rules

Now, you'd think that **Truth Social would be the wild west**—a place where people could post **anything.**

Wrong. **There are rules.**

- **You cannot criticize Trump.**
- **You cannot mention that Trump lost the election.**
- **You cannot post anything that makes Trump sad.**

It's like **North Korea, but with worse graphics.**

Within **days,** people start getting **banned from Truth Social.**

BANNED. FROM TRUTH SOCIAL.

People who were too extreme for **Truth Social.**

A place where **insane conspiracy theories are welcome** but **mild criticism of Trump gets you permanently exiled.**

Some guy posted:

"Hey, maybe Trump should just let the election thing go."

BOOM. ACCOUNT DELETED.

Some woman dared to say:

"Hey, this website doesn't work very well."

BOOM. GONE.

At this point, **even Trump supporters are like,** **"Wait, didn't we hate censorship?"**

Act IV: Trump's Posts – A Masterclass in Digital Nonsense

Now, let's talk about **the main attraction.**

The reason **anyone even logs onto this website.**

Trump's posts.

Because, oh boy, **does this man POST.**

Twitter Trump was **bad.** But **Truth Social Trump?**

FULLY UNHINGED.

This man is **ranting daily.** He is **posting like a guy who just discovered social media yesterday.**

Every morning, he wakes up, grabs his phone, and **furiously types like a raccoon on Adderall.**

Here are some **actual Truth Social posts:**

- **"DO NOT TRUST THE FAKE NEWS! THEY SAY I LOST! I DID NOT! I AM STILL PRESIDENT IN MY HEART!"**
- **"BIDEN IS A DISASTER! EVEN HIS DOG HATES HIM!"**
- **"I INVENTED THE WORD 'TREMENDOUS.' LOOK IT UP!"**

Folks, **this is not a world leader.**

This is your weird uncle who drinks too much at Thanksgiving and starts ranting about UFOs.

And the best part?

NOBODY IS THERE TO STOP HIM.

No Twitter fact-checkers.

No aides telling him, **"Sir, maybe don't post that."**

Just **pure, unfiltered Trump madness.**

It's like **watching a car crash, but the car is orange,** and instead of airbags, it just tweets conspiracy theories.

Act V: The Future of Truth Social – Or, How to Lose Millions in Record Time

Fast forward to **2023.**

Is Truth Social the biggest social media site ever?

No.

Is it even the second-biggest?

No.

Is it **barely surviving, losing money faster than Trump's casinos?**

YES.

Investors start **pulling out.**

The stock value **tanks.**

Even **Trump stops posting as much.**

At this point, Truth Social is like **a ghost town where the only remaining users are bots and that one guy who still thinks JFK Jr. is coming back.**

Meanwhile, Trump is on stage at a rally, still screaming:

"TRUTH SOCIAL IS THE GREATEST SOCIAL MEDIA PLATFORM! EVERYONE LOVES IT! EVEN ELON MUSK IS JEALOUS!"

Sir.

Even your own fans are back on Twitter.

It's over. Let it go.

Final Thoughts: The Dumbest Social Media Site in History

Truth Social will go down in history as **one of the most ridiculous tech failures ever.**

- **It was built out of spite.**

- **It was run like a high school group project where nobody did the work.**

- **It banned its own users for saying things that were too honest.**

And in the end? **It accomplished nothing.**

Twitter is still standing.

Facebook is still standing.

Even MySpace is probably still hanging on somehow.

But **Truth Social?**

DOA.

And honestly? **That seems about right.**

Chapter 12:

Biden, Obama, and Hillary – The Trump Obsession

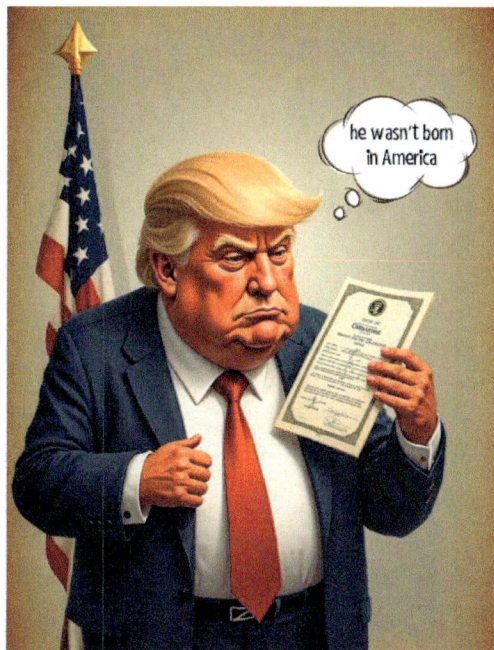

Ah, obsessions! Some people obsess over **sports teams, celebrities, or that one text message they sent at 2 AM that they can never unsend.**

But Donald J. Trump? Oh no, folks. **This man is OBSESSED with three people like a raccoon is obsessed with digging through your trash at 3 AM.**

- Joe Biden? "SLEEPY JOE! WORST PRESIDENT EVER! VERY LOW ENERGY!"

- Barack Obama? "TOTAL DISASTER! TOOK ALL THE CREDIT! MAYBE NOT EVEN AMERICAN!"

- Hillary Clinton? "CROOKED! SHOULD BE IN JAIL! WHY IS SHE NOT IN JAIL?!"

This isn't **normal political rivalry.**

This is **full-on, tinfoil-hat, restraining-order levels of obsession.**

The man lost the presidency in 2020, and he is STILL screaming about these three people like they stole his lunch money in high school.

So sit back, grab some popcorn, and prepare yourself for **the wildest, most unhinged, most ALL-CAPS meltdown in history.**

Act I: The Biden Breakdown – Or, How Trump Became a Human Twitter Thread

Now, let's start with **Joe Biden,** a man so mild-mannered, he looks like he was created in a lab to sell comfortable sneakers to grandpas.

You'd think, after losing to Biden, Trump would just **move on.**

Find **a new target.**

Start yelling at **windmills again.**

NOPE.

Trump is STILL raging about Joe Biden like a guy who got dumped and just can't let it go.

• **"SLEEPY JOE IS RUINING AMERICA!"**

• **"BIDEN HAS NO ENERGY! NO STAMINA! PROBABLY CAN'T EVEN LIFT A CHAIR!"**

• **"I HAD THE GREATEST ECONOMY EVER! BIDEN IS A DISASTER! WORST IN HISTORY!"**

Sir.

It has been YEARS.

You sound like a guy who still brings up his ex at every dinner party.

Somewhere in Delaware, **Biden is peacefully eating ice cream, unaware that Trump is pacing back and forth in Mar-a-Lago, frothing at the mouth like a rabid Cheeto.**

Act II: The Obama Obsession – Or, "WHY IS EVERYONE STILL TALKING ABOUT HIM?!"

Oh, folks, now we get to **the real rage-fueled meltdown.**

Donald J. Trump **HATES** Barack Obama.

Why? Because **Obama is everything Trump isn't.**

- **Charismatic?** Check.

- **Well-spoken?** Check.

- **Respected worldwide?** Check.

- **Able to finish a sentence without sounding like a malfunctioning Roomba?** Big check.

From the moment Trump **descended that golden escalator** like a budget supervillain, he has been **screaming about Obama** louder than a drunk guy at a sports bar.

"OBAMA SPYED ON ME!"

"OBAMA STOLE ALL THE CREDIT!"

"OBAMA'S BIRTH CERTIFICATE – VERY SUSPICIOUS!"

Sir.

Barack Obama has been living his best life, going on Netflix deals and kite-surfing with billionaires.

He is not thinking about you.

Meanwhile, Trump is **losing sleep at night, ranting about how Obama once got a bigger applause than he did.**

At this point, **if Michelle Obama posts a picture of their dog, Trump probably starts screaming into his pillow.**

Act III: Hillary Clinton – The Woman Who Lives in Trump's Head Rent-Free

And now, **the FINAL BOSS.**

HILLARY. RODHAM. CLINTON.

It has been **eight years since 2016, and Trump is STILL SCREAMING ABOUT HER.**

EIGHT. YEARS.

- **"CROOKED HILLARY!"**
- **"LOCK HER UP!"**
- **"WHY IS SHE NOT IN JAIL?"**

Sir.

She is writing books, sipping wine, and ignoring your nonsense.

She moved on. **YOU DIDN'T.**

Trump still **brings up Hillary at rallies**, at interviews, at **random breakfast buffets** where no one even asked.

Waiter: "Sir, would you like eggs or pancakes?"

Trump: "LET ME TELL YOU ABOUT CROOKED HILLARY!"

At this point, **even his own supporters are tired of it.**

One guy in the back of a rally whispers, **"Wait... I thought we were supposed to be mad at Biden now?"**

Act IV: The Greatest Meltdowns – A Collection of Trump's Best Rants

And now, folks, let's take a look at **Trump's greatest meltdowns about Biden, Obama, and Hillary.**

Because this man **doesn't just dislike them—he has MONOLOGUES.**

THE TIME HE CHALLENGED BIDEN TO A FIGHT

At a rally, Trump **randomly** says:

"If I had to fight Joe Biden, I would knock him out in 2 seconds. Very weak. Very frail!"

Sir.

You are a 77-year-old man.

This is not WrestleMania.

You do NOT need to fight Joe Biden.

Meanwhile, **Biden is eating pudding somewhere, completely unaware** that Trump just challenged him to a UFC match.

THE TIME HE WANTED TO ERASE OBAMA FROM HISTORY

Trump, upset that **people still liked Obama,** decides:

"WE SHOULD REMOVE HIS NAME FROM ALL BUILDINGS!"

Yes, folks. This man wanted to **airbrush Obama out of history** like a bad ex-boyfriend deleting selfies.

Sir, that is **not how history works.**

This isn't The Sims. You can't just delete people.

THE TIME HE SAID HILLARY CLINTON CONTROLLED EVERYTHING

One time, Trump **claimed Hillary Clinton ran "a secret global crime syndicate."**

Sir.

She couldn't even win Wisconsin.

You think she runs THE WHOLE WORLD?

Act V: The Never-Ending Obsession

Here we are, folks. **It's 2027, and Trump is STILL RANTING.**

At this point, even his own **supporters are exhausted.**

- **"Sir, Hillary isn't running anymore."**
- **"Sir, Obama is retired."**
- **"Sir, Joe Biden is literally asleep."**

And what does Trump do?

DOES HE MOVE ON?

NOPE.

He just **keeps screaming into the void, hoping someone will still listen.**

Meanwhile, Joe Biden **is out biking.**

Obama **is on vacation.**

Hillary **is drinking a nice glass of wine.**

And Trump? **Still pacing, still ranting, still tweeting into his failed social media platform.**

It's over, sir.

Let. It. Go.

Final Thoughts: The Most Pathetic Obsession in Political History

This man lost an election **years ago** and is STILL screaming about it.

At this point, even **his own supporters are checking their watches, waiting for him to talk about something new.**

But no. **This is it. This is the hill he dies on.**

And honestly? **That seems about right.**

Chapter 13:

World Leaders, Rocket Men, and Love Letters from Kim

Ah, diplomacy! That ancient, noble art of **talking things out like grown-ups instead of flinging nukes at each other like toddlers with firecrackers.**

For most presidents, diplomacy means **long meetings, careful negotiations, and making sure nobody** accidentally starts World War III over a bad handshake.

For Donald J. Trump?

Diplomacy means sending weird tweets, talking about his "chemistry" with dictators, and treating global politics like a reality TV show.

This man **didn't just meet with world leaders—he COLLECTED them.** Like **Pokémon,** but instead of **Pikachu,** it was Putin, Xi Jinping, and that one time he fell in love with **Kim Jong-Un.**

Yes, folks.

Trump **wrote love letters** to the Supreme Leader of North Korea.

Let that sink in.

This is not a drill.

So grab your passports, pack your emotional support whiskey, and prepare for a **wild trip around the world with the most unqualified travel guide in history.**

Act I: Putin – The Best Friend He's Never Met?

Let's start with **Vladimir Putin**, the shirtless horseback-riding, bear-wrestling **Bond villain of Russia.**

Most U.S. presidents are **suspicious of Russia.**

Trump? **Trump LOVES Russia.**

- **"Putin is very strong, very powerful, very respected!"**
- **"Maybe we should be friends with Russia!"**
- **"He said he didn't meddle in the election, and I believe him!"**

Sir.

The CIA, FBI, and every U.S. intelligence agency says Russia hacked the election.

But you believe Putin?

At this point, **even his own advisors are staring at the floor, pretending they don't exist.**

Putin, meanwhile, is probably sitting in his palace, sipping vodka, petting a hairless cat, thinking, **"This is too easy."**

Act II: Xi Jinping – "Maybe Being a Dictator for Life Isn't a Bad Idea?"

Now let's talk about **China.**

Every president before Trump? **Tough on China. Lots of rules, lots of trade policies.**

Trump? **ABSOLUTELY ENCHANTED BY XI JINPING.**

At one point, **China literally changed its laws so Xi Jinping could stay president for life.**

And what does Trump say?

"WOW! PRESIDENT FOR LIFE? MAYBE WE SHOULD TRY THAT IN AMERICA!"

SIR. THAT IS LITERALLY A DICTATORSHIP.

At this point, **Thomas Jefferson wakes up in his grave, slaps himself in the face, and goes back to sleep.**

Act III: The G7 Summit – Trump vs. The Entire Free World

Ah, the **G7 Summit.**

A time for **leaders of the world's biggest economies to meet, shake hands, and pretend they like each other.**

For most presidents? **Serious, professional, respectful.**

For Trump? **A chance to throw a tantrum, storm out early, and start a trade war with Canada.**

CANADA.

THE NICEST COUNTRY ON EARTH.

At one point, **Trump literally calls Justin Trudeau "very dishonest and weak."**

Sir.

You just picked a fight with a country whose national sport is apologizing.

Trudeau is over here, sipping maple syrup, looking confused, like **"Did I miss something?"**

Meanwhile, **Angela Merkel is rubbing her temples like a mom dealing with a screaming toddler in a grocery store.**

The rest of the world is **trying to negotiate climate change policies.**

Trump? **Trump is yelling about how much he loves coal.**

And then, when everyone **tries to get a group handshake for the cameras,** Trump just **crosses his arms like a kid who didn't get ice cream and refuses to play.**

That's it. **That's his entire strategy.**

Act IV: Kim Jong-Un – The World's Strangest Bromance

And now, folks, we arrive at **THE MAIN EVENT.**

Trump vs. Kim Jong-Un.

The most **chaotic** and **unhinged** relationship in modern history.

At first, it's **PURE HATRED.**

- **"LITTLE ROCKET MAN!"**

- **"I HAVE A BIGGER NUCLEAR BUTTON!"**

- **"NORTH KOREA WILL BE TOTALLY DESTROYED!"**

Kim Jong-Un is probably **scrolling through Twitter in his bunker, screaming into a pillow.**

And then—**A MIRACLE.**

Trump and Kim **meet in person.**

Suddenly, **Trump is in love.**

"WE HAVE GREAT CHEMISTRY!"

"KIM JONG-UN IS A VERY TALENTED MAN!"

"WE FELL IN LOVE!"

FELL IN LOVE?!

Sir, **this is a nuclear-armed dictator.**

Not a contestant on The Bachelor.

AND THEN IT GETS WEIRDER.

Kim **sends Trump actual love letters.**

And Trump? **KEEPS THEM.** Like a **teenager saving texts from their crush.**

"THESE LETTERS ARE BEAUTIFUL! LOVE LETTERS!"

Sir.

You are the President of the United States, not a middle schooler writing poetry in the margins of your history textbook.

Meanwhile, **Kim is probably showing these letters to his generals, saying, "This guy is an idiot."**

Act V: Trump at the United Nations – The Worst Stand-Up Routine Ever

Ah, the **United Nations General Assembly.**

A room full of **world leaders giving speeches about serious global issues.**

And Trump?

Trump **gets on stage and says:**

"I HAVE DONE MORE THAN ANY PRESIDENT IN HISTORY!"

AND THE WHOLE ROOM **BURSTS OUT LAUGHING.**

A ROOM FULL OF WORLD LEADERS **JUST LAUGHED AT HIM.**

And Trump? **He is SHOCKED.**

He **thought they were cheering.**

Sir.

They are LAUGHING AT YOU, NOT WITH YOU.

Final Thoughts: The Most Embarrassing Foreign Policy in History

Most presidents **build alliances.**

Most presidents **try to keep peace.**

Trump? **Trump collects dictators like Pokémon cards.**

And in the end?

NOTHING GOT DONE.

Putin? **Still Putin.**

China? **Still China.**

North Korea? **Still North Korea.**

And Trump?

Still pacing around Mar-a-Lago, writing love letters to Kim Jong-Un, and wondering why nobody takes him seriously.

And honestly? **That seems about right.**

Chapter 14:

The 2024 Election and the Never-Ending Sore Loser Tour

Ah, elections! The grand American tradition of **long lines, malfunctioning voting machines, and campaign ads so painful you'd rather watch a 24-hour marathon of infomercials about foot fungus cream.**

Every four years, Americans gather at polling stations to do their civic duty, which is **choosing between two old men who look like they've been awake since the Civil War.**

For most presidential candidates, **if you lose, you shake hands, give a nice speech, and go home to write a book that nobody reads.**

For Donald J. Trump? **OH, NO.**

When Trump loses an election, **he doesn't just accept it and move on.**

Oh, no, folks! **HE DECLARES WAR ON REALITY.**

- **"THE ELECTION WAS STOLEN!"**

- **"MASSIVE FRAUD! BIGGEST SCANDAL IN HISTORY!"**

- **"I ACTUALLY WON! I'M STILL PRESIDENT!"**

Sir.

It has been **FOUR YEARS.**

You are not president. You are a guy in Florida screaming at a golf cart.

So grab some popcorn, folks, because we are about to take **a front-row seat** to the most **insane, unhinged, all-caps-rant-fueled comeback attempt in political history.**

Act I: The Announcement – Or, The Moment Everyone Pretended to Be Excited

It's **November 2022.**

Trump has been **out of office for two years,** but does he move on?

NOPE.

Instead, he **marches onto a stage at Mar-a-Lago,** chest puffed out, spray tan cranked up to "nuclear Cheeto," and **announces he is running AGAIN.**

And the crowd?

Dead silence.

Even his most loyal fans are like:

"Wait… we're doing this again?"

Melania is standing there, blinking in Morse code for help.

Ivanka is **sipping her drink like she just realized she has to pretend to support him for another four years.**

Eric Trump is **clapping like he just learned how.**

And Trump, of course, **acts like he just cured cancer.**

"PEOPLE ARE SAYING THIS IS THE GREATEST ANNOUNCEMENT OF ALL TIME!"

Sir.

Your audience looks like they'd rather be anywhere else.

Act II: The Rally Circuit – The Same Old Hits, But With Extra Bitterness

Now, folks, when a normal politician **runs for president again,** they come up with **new ideas.**

Not Trump!

Trump's **2024 campaign is the greatest hits tour of his 2016 and 2020 rants.**

The man is out here giving the SAME speeches he's been giving for EIGHT YEARS.

- **"BUILD THE WALL!"** (Sir, the wall was never finished.)

- **"LOCK HER UP!"** (Sir, Hillary Clinton has been retired for years.)

- **"CROOKED MEDIA!"** (Sir, they're still covering you because you keep saying crazy things.)

It's like watching an **aging rock star who refuses to release new music.**

At this point, **even his fans have to pretend they're still excited.**

"Yeah, woo, **lock her up**... I guess?"

Act III: The Debates – Or, The Part Where Trump Starts Swinging at the Air

Ah, presidential debates!

A time for **candidates to present their ideas,** answer questions, and **try not to look like a complete mess.**

For Trump? **DEBATES ARE CAGE MATCHES.**

He **doesn't answer questions.**

He **yells over everyone.**

He **insults his opponent like he's doing a roast battle at a comedy club.**

At one point, **Biden sighs and rubs his forehead, looking like a grandpa who just got locked out of his iPhone again.**

The moderator tries to keep control, but Trump is just **flailing his arms, shouting random words like a malfunctioning parrot.**

- **"HUNTER BIDEN LAPTOP!"**
- **"BIGGEST ECONOMY EVER!"**
- **"FAKE NEWS!"**
- **"JOE IS SLEEPY! VERY SLEEPY!"**

Sir.

None of this answers the question.

The moderators are **trying to fact-check him in real-time, but it's like trying to correct a tornado.**

At one point, **Trump interrupts Biden so much, they have to mute his mic.**

And Trump? **Starts yelling at the air.**

He is debating HIMSELF.

And the MAGA crowd? **LOVES IT.**

They're **cheering like he just won WrestleMania.**

At this point, **Biden just stares into the camera like Jim from The Office.**

Act IV: The Election Night Meltdown – The Sequel No One Wanted

Ah, election night 2024.

Americans go to bed **thinking they'll wake up and finally have closure.**

WRONG.

Because just like 2020, **Trump declares victory BEFORE the votes are even counted.**

He **marches onto stage**, holds up a thumbs-up, and shouts:

"WE WON! IN A LANDSLIDE! THANK YOU, EVERYONE!"

Meanwhile, **news anchors are sweating bullets, holding up maps, trying to explain that NO, SIR, THE ELECTION IS NOT OVER.**

And when the final numbers roll in and **Trump loses AGAIN?**

OH, THE MELTDOWN.

- **"STOLEN! WORST SCANDAL EVER!"**

- **"MAIL-IN BALLOTS? TOTALLY RIGGED!"**

- **"FAKE VOTES! FAKE VOTES EVERYWHERE!"**

Sir.

You lost AGAIN.

Go home. Play golf. Take up knitting. **SOMETHING.**

But no.

He SUES.

Again.

He rants on **Truth Social.**

Again.

He calls for **"recounts in states he never even campaigned in."**

At this point, **even Rudy Giuliani is tired.**

Even **Fox News is like, "Dude, please, let it go."**

And the Supreme Court?

They take one look at Trump's legal case and say:

"Sir, we are not reading this. Please stop faxing us napkins covered in Sharpie writing."

Act V: The Final Meltdown – Or, The Never-Ending Sore Loser Tour

Now, folks, you'd THINK that **after losing TWICE,** Trump would just **go away.**

NOPE.

HE STARTS HIS "STOLEN ELECTION" TOUR.

This man is out here **holding rallies in empty parking lots, ranting about fraud, selling T-shirts that say "TRUMP 2028: THIRD TIME'S THE CHARM!"**

His fans are **standing there in lawn chairs, nodding, pretending they still believe him.**

"Yeah, woo… stolen election… I guess?"

Meanwhile, Biden is **trying to govern,** and Trump is still **holding up a piece of paper that says '100 MILLION FAKE VOTES!' drawn in crayon.**

At this point, the **entire country is exhausted.**

- **Democrats are exhausted.**
- **Republicans are exhausted.**
- **Even Trump's lawyers are exhausted.**

And Trump?

Still pacing, still yelling, still tweeting into the void.

Sir. Please. We beg you. Take a nap.

Final Thoughts: The Election That Will Never End

Trump lost.

Twice.

And yet, somehow, **we are STILL TALKING ABOUT IT.**

At this point, even his own supporters are looking at their watches, waiting for him to just… **stop.**

But will he?

Oh no, folks.

HE'S NEVER STOPPING.

And honestly?

That seems about right.

Chapter 15:

The Dump That Never Ends

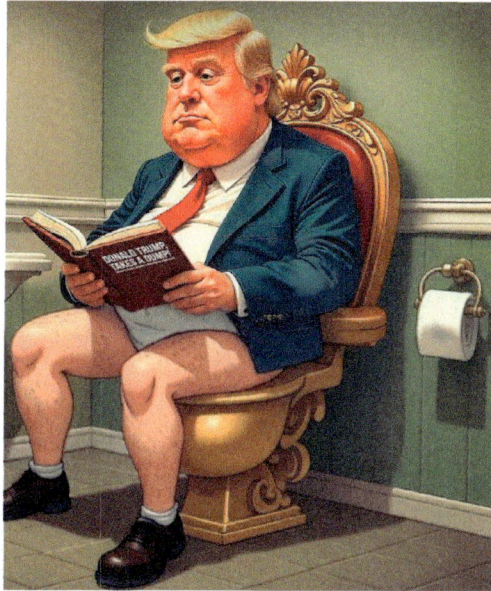

Ah, America! Land of the free, home of the brave, and currently being held hostage by **a spray-tanned game show host with the IQ of a potato.**

Folks, we've laughed, we've cried (mostly from laughter), and we've watched as one man turned **the most powerful office in the world into a stand-up special that nobody asked for.**

But here's the thing: **This isn't just a joke anymore.**

This is **real.**

This is **scary.**

This is **America on the brink of turning into the world's biggest episode of Survivor, but instead of voting people off the island, Trump just shouts "WITCH HUNT!" until they resign.**

And as we sit here, watching the orange madness unfold, we have to ask ourselves:

How bad can it really get?

Oh, folks.

Buckle up.

Act I: The Idiot King – Or, How America Elected a Twitter Troll

We used to elect **leaders.** People who could at least **pretend to be competent.**

But somehow, we went from **George Washington crossing the Delaware** to **Donald Trump rage-tweeting about the deep state while sitting on a golden toilet.**

How did we get here?

- One part reality TV culture.

- One part Facebook conspiracy theories.

- One giant steaming pile of political apathy.

And now? **America is being run like a failing casino.**

- The economy? **Rigged.**

- Foreign policy? **Bankrupt.**

- The Constitution? **Thrown into a shredder and replaced with tweets.**

At this point, if **Trump accidentally nuked Canada,** he'd just look into the camera and say:

"FAKE NEWS! NEVER HAPPENED! CANADA WAS A DISASTER ANYWAY!"

And somehow, **40% of Americans would still clap.**

Act II: The Chaos Presidency – Or, Why Every Morning Feels Like a Dumpster Fire

Remember when **you could wake up in the morning and NOT worry that the president did something insane overnight?**

NOT ANYMORE.

Every single day under Trump is like waking up in **a burning building where the only way out is blocked by Rudy Giuliani.**

- **"Trump just declared war on Denmark."**
- **"Trump accidentally called the Queen of England 'babe' during a state dinner."**
- **"Trump thinks California is a foreign country."**

And every time the news breaks, **the entire planet does a collective facepalm.**

It's gotten so bad that when Trump says something **insane,** we don't even react anymore.

We just go, **"Yeah, that sounds about right."**

The bar is **so low, it's underground.**

Act III: The America We're Leaving Behind – And It Ain't Pretty

Now, let's get serious for a second.

Because while it's fun to **laugh at the madness,** we also have to **realize where this is all heading.**

America isn't just becoming a joke. **It's becoming a cautionary tale.**

- The rich are getting richer, the poor are getting poorer.

- Education? Cut.

- Healthcare? A disaster.

- Climate change? Apparently fake.

And while Trump is out here **screaming about Hillary's emails for the 4,000th time,** real problems are piling up like unpaid bills.

We are watching **democracy crumble in real-time.**

And here's the scariest part:

The next Trump could be even worse.

Act IV: The Road to Authoritarianism – Or, How a Dictator is Born

Let's break it down:

1. **First, you attack the press.**

   - **"Fake news! The media is the enemy of the people!"**

   - Now, half the country **doesn't believe facts exist anymore.**

2. **Then, you go after the courts.**

- "The justice system is rigged! Witch hunt!"
- Now, the law **only applies to your enemies.**

3. **Then, you mess with elections.**

   - "Rigged! Fraud! Only I can be trusted!"
   - Now, you've **convinced millions that** democracy is fake.

At this point, **congratulations! You're officially a dictator!**

Trump isn't just **a bad president.** He's **a test run for** something much worse.

A **smarter version of Trump?**

That's **terrifying.**

Act V: The Future We're Facing – Or, How Bad Could It Really Get?

You think it's bad now? **Just wait.**

Trump's second term, if he gets it?
- A full-blown police state.
- Journalists locked up.

- Protesters tear-gassed.

- Constitution rewritten in crayon.

Imagine **Trump on TV, smiling like a used car salesman, saying:**

"GOOD NEWS, FOLKS! I'M PRESIDENT FOR LIFE! HUGE WIN! EVERYONE'S SAYING IT!"

And the worst part?

Half of America would cheer.

The other half would just **pack their bags and start Googling 'how to move to Canada.'**

Act VI: The Final Warning – Or, WAKE UP, AMERICA!

Here's the deal, folks.

Trump **isn't the problem.**

He's the symptom.

The real problem? **America is letting this happen.**

We're letting **politicians get dumber.**

We're letting **corporations take over.**

We're letting **conspiracies replace common sense.**

This is how democracies die.

Not with a bang, but with **a bunch of idiots chanting "LOCK HER UP" while their country burns to the ground.**

At this point, even **George Orwell is looking down** from the afterlife, shaking his head, saying, "I warned you morons."

Final Thoughts: The Dump That Never Ends

Trump may be gone someday.

But the **damage he did?**

That's going to last for decades.

- The **political circus?** Still here.

- The **conspiracies?** Still here.

- The **deep distrust in government?** Still here.

And as long as **people keep falling for this nonsense,** America will keep sliding further into **a giant, flaming, fast-food-filled abyss.**

So what can we do?

Simple:

STOP ELECTING REALITY TV HOSTS TO RUN A COUNTRY.

Because if we don't?

Well…

The dump will never end.

And honestly?

That seems about right.

Printed in Dunstable, United Kingdom